To all of my niblings, who make my world shine bright.
—T. B.

To Amitai and Boaz, best brothers ever.
—A. L.

Workman Kids
Workman Publishing
Hachette Book Group, Inc.
1290 Avenue of the Americas
New York, NY 10104
workman.com

Workman Kids is an imprint of Workman Publishing, a division of Hachette Book Group, Inc.
The Workman name and logo are registered trademarks of Hachette Book Group, Inc.

Design by Daniella Graner

The publisher is not responsible for websites (or their content) that are not owned by the publisher.

Workman books may be purchased in bulk for business, educational, or promotional use. For information, please contact your local bookseller or the Hachette Book Group Special Markets Department at special.markets@hbgusa.com.

Library of Congress Cataloging-in-Publication Data is available.

ISBN 978-1-5235-3016-8

First Edition: September 2025

Distributed in Europe by Hachette Livre, 58 rue Jean Bleuzen, 92 178 Vanves Cedex, France.
Distributed in the United Kingdom by Hachette UK Ltd., Carmelite House, 50 Victoria Embankment, London EC4Y 0DZ.

Made in Dongguan, China (APS) 06/25

10 9 8 7 6 5 4 3 2 1

Twinkle, Twinkle, HANUKKAH

Words by
Talia Benamy

Art by
Aura Lewis

Twinkle, twinkle, menorah,
on this happy Hanukkah
with the candles burning bright,
giving us their cheerful light.

Twinkle, twinkle, menorah,
on this happy Hanukkah.

Brightly, brightly, candles shine.
The shamash lights them in line.

By the window they reside,
spreading light both far and wide.

**Spinning, spinning, round and round,
with our dreidels on the ground.**

**Play a game and win some gelt.
Just don't let the chocolate melt!**

Sharing, sharing, one and all—
lots of presents, big and small.

Books and games, a toy, a glove.
Gifts for everyone we love.

Sizzle, sizzle in the pan.
Grab a latke while we can.

Right on top we'll spread across sour cream or applesauce.

Yummy, yummy, tasty treat!
Sufganiyot for us to eat.

Jelly doughnuts made in oil,
gobbled up before they spoil.

Singing, singing, slow and fast,
songs with stories of our past.
Celebrate our history,
our people and their victory.

**Mighty, mighty Maccabees
fought the Greeks and won with ease.**

**They saved the temple and the Jews,
then found oil they could use.**

Grateful, grateful we all are
that our people got this far.

**Miracles for all to see
set the Jewish people free.**

Happy, happy we will be
with neighbors, friends, and family.

**Near or far or in between,
in one room or on a screen.**

Jews around the world all share our traditions everywhere.

**Chag sameach, all eight nights,
with the twinkling candles' lights.**

**Twinkle, twinkle, menorah,
on this happy Hanukkah.**

Hanukkah is a celebration of Jewish survival.

More than two thousand years ago, the Greek Empire took control of the land of Israel, where the Jewish people lived. The Greeks wanted to stop the Jews from practicing their religion and their traditions. They even damaged the temple in Jerusalem, which was one of the Jews' main places to gather.

The Jewish people didn't just give up, though. They knew they wanted to stand up for themselves, so a group of Jewish warriors called the Maccabees fought back. They took control of the temple and kicked the Greeks out. And then, as the story goes, they tried to find oil to light the menorah, the beautiful candelabra that had always lit up the temple. They were able to find only a very small amount of oil in the wreckage that the Greeks had left behind—enough for a single day. But somehow, that small amount of oil miraculously lasted for eight whole days.

Today, we celebrate Hanukkah each year to remember the miracle of that oil and of our survival against all odds. We light our menorahs using a shamash, or helper candle, to light the others, often near windows so we can spread the light out into the world. We eat foods that are fried in oil, like latkes, a Yiddish word that means potato pancakes, and sufganiyot, the Hebrew word for jelly doughnuts. We play games with dreidels, spinning tops with Hebrew letters on them that describe the miracle that happened so long ago. We give gifts to one another, sometimes in the form of gelt, which are yummy chocolate coins. And we sing songs about the story of Hanukkah and the miracle of our people's victory as we wish each other a chag sameach—happy holiday!